LISTEN!

A Million Children's Voices in Scotland

© Save the Children

First published in 2000 by:
Glowworm Books Ltd, Unit 7, Greendykes Industrial Estate,
Broxburn, West Lothian, EH52 6PG, Scotland

Telephone: 01506-857570
Fax: 01506-858100
E-mail: admin@glowwormbooks.co.uk
URL: http://www.glowwormbooks.co.uk

On behalf of:
Save the Children, Haymarket House, 8 Clifton Terrace
Edinburgh, EH12 5DR

Telephone: 0131-527-8200
Fax: 0131-527-8201

ISBN 1 87151262 2

Printed and bound by Scotprint, Haddington.

Reprint Code   10 9   8   7   6   5   4   3   2   1

Introduction

There are over one million children under the age of 18 in Scotland today.

What are their thoughts and ideas, fears and concerns, hopes and dreams?

Too often children's feelings and opinions are not heard. *Save the Children's Million Children* Campaign gives Scotland's children and young people the chance to have their say on life for them in Scotland at 2000.

Listen! A Million Children's Voices in Scotland is a unique living history book of children and young people's stories, drawings, poems, designs, cartoons and manifestos for the 21st century. The material reflects their values, their feelings about their family and community and their visions for the future.

Together, the written and visual material demonstrates the innovative and creative ideas of Scotland's young citizens at the start of a new millennium.

Contents

Community

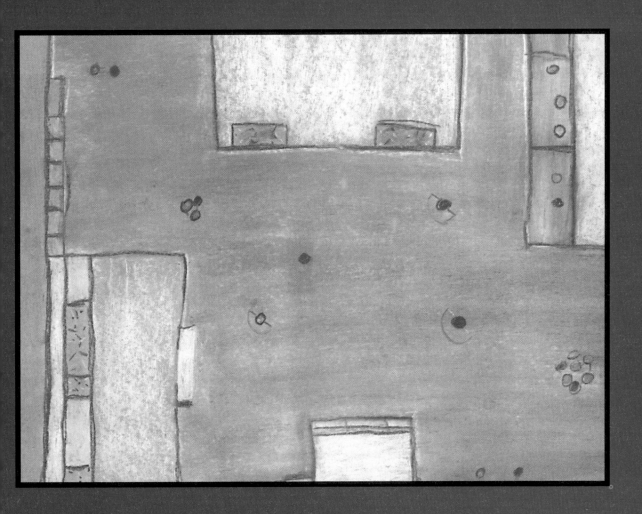

Stephanie Sunley *Ellon Primary School, Ellon*

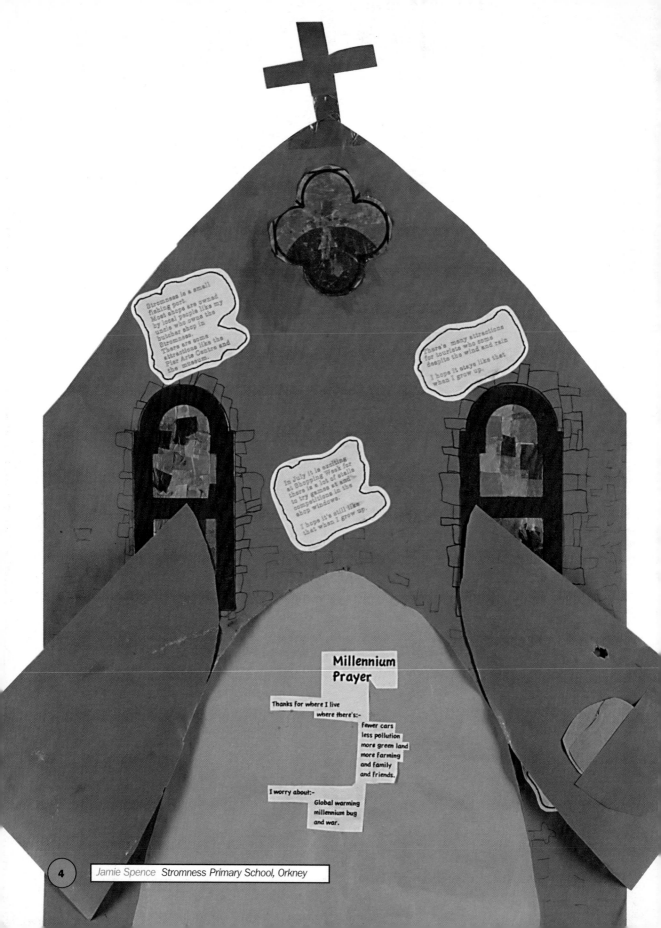

Stromness is a small fishing port. Most shops are owned by local people like my uncle who owns the butcher shop in Stromness.
There are some attractions like the Pier Arts Centre and the museum.

There's many attractions for tourists who come despite the wind and rain

I hope it stays like that when I grow up.

In July it is exciting at Shopping Week for there is a lot of stalls to try games at and competitions in the shop windows.

I hope it's still like that when I grow up.

Millennium Prayer

Thanks for where I live
where there's:-
fewer cars
less pollution
more green land
more farming
and family
and friends.

I worry about:-
Global warming
millennium bug
and war.

Jamie Spence Stromness Primary School, Orkney

MY LIFE IN ORKNEY

A Swimming pool in Orkney

The streets of Stromness are winding and narrow.

Planes not expencive

NO WORLD WAR

FUTURE CAR

MAINLAND

Try and get less [pol]lution

Fast Speeding Boats

Tunnel in between Scotland and Orkney

less disasters

David Stockon Stromness Primary School, Orkney

5

PENTLAND FIRTH TUNNEL

WHAT CAN BE DONE TO USE ORKNEY BETTER

There should be a Pentland Firth Tunnel from the Island of Hoy to
Thurso because flights cost loads of money and boat trips take ages.

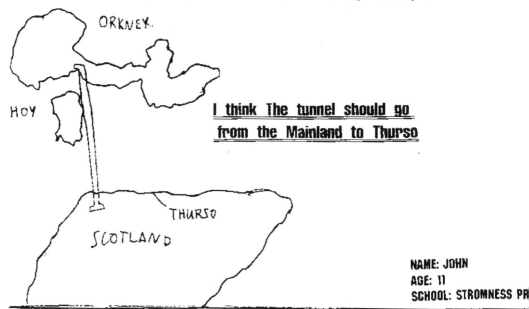

ORKNEY

HOY

**I think The tunnel should go
from the Mainland to Thurso**

THURSO

SCOTLAND

NAME: JOHN
AGE: 11
SCHOOL: STROMNESS PR

BIGGER AIRPORT IN ORKNEY

There should be a bigger airport in Orkney because there is miles and
miles of spare land beside the airport and it could be used to build a
bigger airport and a bigger runway, so jumbo jets can land in Orkney.

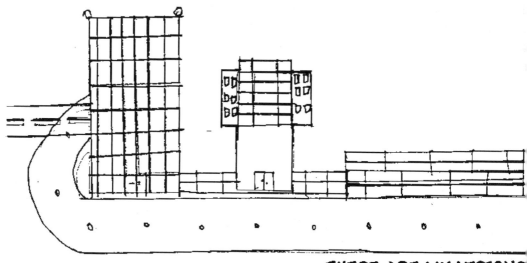

THESE ARE MY VISIONS

OIL PROTECTION BRIDGE IN ORKNEY
WAVE POWER

CHANGES IN ORKNEY

There should be wave power in Orkney because we get lots of waves from the west of the Atlantic Ocean. And the oil rigs out east of Orkney might be leaking and nothing can be done about all of the oil floating into Orkney, so Orkney should get some sort of oil protection bridge around it.

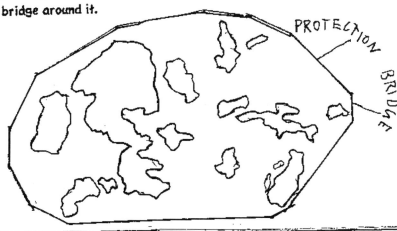

HIGH SPEED TRAINS AROUND ORKNEY
MORE BUILDING EQUIPMENT

he land should also be used to build high speed trains because it ould be cheaper than going in a car and it wouldn't skid off the road ke other cars, so we could save more children that would have been illed on the road. The towns of Stromness and Kirkwall are all too rammed together so they should be spread out more. I think Orkney hould get more building equipment to smoothen out the roads that aven't been tarmaced for years!

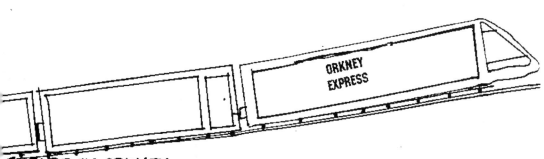

FUTURE IN ORKNEY

I was born in East Calder and lived their till I was one. I moved away for a while but I moved back when I was six.

Even though all my family were born in East Calder we got dirty looks I am now twelve and I some times get dirty looks when I walk to the shops.

The street where I live has the worst Reputation in East Calder.

Every one is so nosy they're always interested in other peoples business. All children can do is hang around at the park. After nine o,clock after yts dark people are scared to go out or walking by the shops. Because they're petrofied of what might happen.

Not so long ago I saw a syringe out side the shop, my mum was anoyed because a kid could have jagged their self.

East Calder is not a very friendly or clean village.

Ellana, West Calder

Langbank

Present and Future

by
Fiona and Hannah
Magee Cumming

The shop in the year 1999

The shop in the year 2099

Fiona Magee Hannah Cumming *Langbank Primary School*

Life in Laxdale

I am very lucky to live in Western Isles.I live in a clean environment with a loving family. It is good because we don't ever think we're being stalked or we'll be attacked.Iam lucky because when I go to bed I feel safe, I hear my mum and dad talk .I hear the T.V,the cars going past and dogs.We have great landmarks like the Callanish Stones,the Broch and a memorial for the Iolaire.In our community most people in the town know me and I know them.I go to Laxdale school five days a week.Our teachers are nice to us.I walk home nearly everyday.

I value my parents love ,and the sentimental objects that have been in the family.My friends are nice.My perfect friend would be honest,kind,fair and loyal.I would like it because my friend would be cool.

Iwouldn't like to live in Glasgow because my mother and myself might get hurt.In Stornoway we aren't scared to walk down town.We can go without a second thought about it.On our island we have people from mixed races but we treat them as we treat one another.We don't care what kind of skin they have.I can't understand why people are racist.

It is a beautiful island and we atract many tourists.We do not have much graffiti around Stornoway.There are no car thieves and very little drug abuse.We are very well off on our island.

We have fun things for children too.We have children's clubs.We have clubs for clubbers like The Heb,Twilights,The Legion etc.We have a Sports Centre where you can swim,play tennis,football we also have a gym and a play area.We have the fun hour on Saturdays.We have interesting shops.The best thing about it is the community sprit,because we know each other.We have a carnival every year for charity.So I believe am lucky to be living here.

By
    Ruth MacDonald P.6

Ruth MacDonald Laxdale Primary School, Lewis

My vision of a better barrhead

I dont think it is fair that some people commit crimes and get away them or that some people get blamed for a crime they did not do.

When people get put in prison for something they were said to have done and then when they have served there time they get out of prison and said not guilty. I think this is unfair.

I also think it is not fair when young children or teenagers go into shops and get followed to make sure they dont steal anything all teenagers are not thieves. And I also think there is nothing to do in Barrhead and thats why youngsters get into crime. I think there should be a lot more things to do at night, like the log-in where it is good fun.

There are only about two youth clubs that I know about and there is the log-in café.

There is a lot of young people smoking because there is nothing else to spend there money on. A lot of young people are getting into crime like stealing car badges, smashing windows and stealing because there is not enough to do in Barrhead.

I think to make Barrhead better you would need things like a cinema, Ice-skating and other things teenagers can do at night. The councillors should try to get these things going.

By

Gillian Hanvidge

My Community

My name is Stuart. I was born in Milton in Glasgow but I've lived in different places all over the city. We moved to Pollok around 1993 and moved away on the 4th of November 1998. The reason we moved was because me and my family stayed one up in a "T" close and we used to get a lot of trouble with people hanging about the close.

They used to cover the close with graffiti and it got really bad that you couldn't even walk down the close at night because all of the people hanging about. The other people living in the close were really frightened because of all the trouble.

One time somebody had set fire to the back close and my bedroom was directly above it. When the fire brigade finally put out the fire my bedroom floor was just about to cave in.

The final straw was when my mum was coming out of the close and was attacked - that was hell so we had to move somewhere else.

The good thing about Pollok was that I had lots of friends and I was always having fun. My mum knew all of our neighbours and when it was sunny she used to sit down the back with them drinking tea and enjoying old fashioned chit-chat. We got on really well with everyone and the part of Pollok we stayed in was really nice.

There was another reason I kept moving all the time and this was because of my brother who had a drug addiction and caused a lot of problems.

The biggest problem he caused was when I stayed in Milton. Because my mum didn't give him money he waited until we were sleeping then got one of his friends to set fire to the kitchen curtains. It was the police that moved us out for protection. Today my big brother is fine and clean and stays with his girlfriend and two kids.

We now live in a block of high rise flats, 14 up, in St. Georges Cross in Glasgow. I don't really like staying here because I don't know anyone and the people my age are idiots and just like fighting with the surrounding areas.

There are a lot of different cultures in St. Georges Cross but they never mix. You don't see a white person and coloured person walking down the street together which I think is really sad because at the end of the day they are human except they have darker skin.

The good things about staying in St. Georges Cross is the view from our windows. It's totally amazing. The bus services are good there are so many buses you could get into town and there is a subway which takes you into town in a matter of minutes and it's really cheap.

In the future I hope my mum wins the lottery and moves just outside Glasgow somewhere to a little village which is really peaceful and has no violence. I hope this community would be able to trust one another and not judge anyone by the colour of their skin or the way they were brought up.

In the future I hope everyone will be equal.

Stuart   Age 16

Elaine Hunter Dumbarton Academy, Dumbarton

Love and Relationships

love is a very special word, it is also
a very mature feeling to have for some one.
Love can't be taken for granted and must
be treasured forever.

Anon Dalziel High School, Motherwell

I think that love is a very important word and you have to be very careful how you say it.

Some people say they love each other for the sake of it and they really don't mean it.

I think if you love someone it has to come from the heart and you have to truly, deeply mean it.

Love can mean so many different things.

Some people say love is when you care for someone.

Others say it is when you get a warm, happy feeling inside you when you are close to a person you care for.

Personally I think it is a mixture of these things but I think also it is when you feel close and secure to someone but when you hope nothing bad will ever happen to that certain person you care for.

My Family

My mums name is Linda and my dads name is Gordon. My mum used to go to work but has not retired she has still got many more years to go. She has to stay at home to look after us.She works very hard. My dad works at Friends Ivory and Sime he is an accountant and he works hard and gets money for the family. My brothers name is Fraser he goes to the same school as I do it is called George Watsons College. My brother plays tennis, swimming and much more.

My name is Emma our surname is Humphries. My brother often pulls my hair but I love him. My hobbies are violin, tap dancing, brownies and running. My grandmas name is Anne and my grandads name is Colin. Their surname is Robertson. I love them.

Emma Humphries *George Watson's College, Edinburgh*

LOVE

Love is a very strong & mature word.

Over the world, millions of people enjoy love.

Valentines day, is for showing other people how much you love & care for them.

Everyone has a special love for some one, some time in their life.

Family Values

family are important
They really are the best
And if you'd like to listen
i'll tell you all the rest
I have a little brother
who really is a pain
Sometimes he drives me up the wall
He's making me insane
But nomatter what may happen
Wherever he may be
i'll always love my brother
He means the world to me
And next you have my father
who cannot walk or run
Although he is disabled he
he is alot of fun
he's taught me lots of special things
Which i'll keep within my heart
he's taught me many values
with which i'll never part
And last you have my mother
Whom i love and i adore
And no matter what i do
She'll never shut the door
I know she'll always be there
to lend a helping hand
And even when we argue
I know she understands
And so to all my family
this poem's just for you
And all that i have left to say
Is thank you and i love you

By michelle Seath

Michelle Seath Edinburgh

Ma Life

I wis born in 1986
fae then ma life's
got better.
Ma fear is heights
Ma dream is bein'
a song writer.
Ma hope's to have
a good life.

I wis born in 1986
fae then ma life's
got better.
Ma dream is playin'
fur Rangers
Ma fear is supporting
Celtic.
And ma hope's to have
a good life.

Scotland's a great place to live
Oor families a' live here.
It might be cold,
but that's nae reason no' to like it.

Darren Heaney and *Donna Longburn* Dumbarton Academy, Dumbarton

My Family

I'd like to tell you all about me
And my special family
My mum, my dad, my brother makes three
And then of course there is me.

We live in Borve in Lewis
On an island surrounded by sea
We live there together
My family and me.

I' tell you first about my dad
John Roderick is his name
He works on an oil rig
And so many dads do the same.

He's such a fun-filled person
He cares so much for our family
He always brings home presents
For mum, Connor and me.

And now I'll tell you about my Mum
She really is a lot of fun
She works in school in the office
And she always keeps her promise.

And next I'll tell you about Connor
He really is a good brother
I play with Connor all the time
He really is one of a kind

My name is Warren, I like riding my bike
Playing my computer and playing football
Are things I like
Listening to my stereo, playing with my friends
Can sometimes drive my parents round the bend.

Warren Mackay Airidhantuim Primary School, Isle of Lewis

There are many different kinds and meanings of love. I believe the most common kind of love is unconditional love. This usually occurs in families where the love between a mother and father and their child is unconditional.

Some people say love is when you care about someone a lot, or when you think about someone every second of every day.

I think that love is when you have a warm, happy feeling inside you.

Fiona Thomson **Dalziel High School, Motherwell**

Korina Macleay **Airidhantuim Primary School, Isle of Lewis**

are kind

spend time with you

are helpful

families :

are caring

are loving

Helpful

Friendly

Caring

Always there

Friends are:

Kind

Alistair Boyd Muiredge Primary School, Uddingston

Scotland

3

{NATURE} {AROUND} {ME} {IN} {Scotland}

AS The hills lay Still and the Sky
Slts quit, the birds Sing ther Song,
The tiny blads of glass flicer in the
Soft brese of the cool morning air,
as the flys buzz Past the high tree
tops, the water is falling from the glene
the Smell of the fresh air fill my
nostirls as I then open my eyes
and I See Scotland!

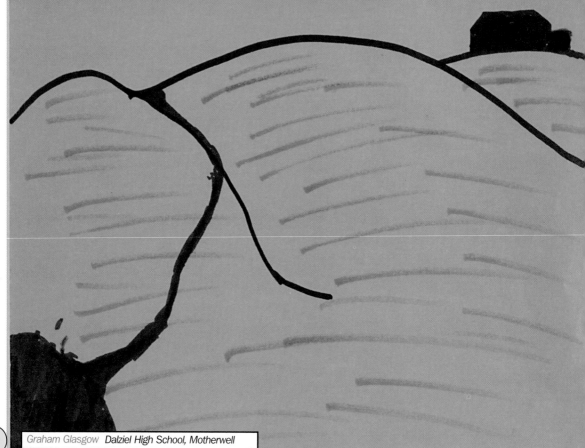

Graham Glasgow Dalziel High School, Motherwell

SCOTLAND'S FUTURE

H
o
p
e
s

&

F
e
a
r
s

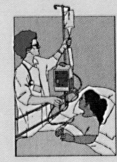

MY HOPES AND FEARS FOR SCOTLAND

My hopes for Scotland are that hospitals and schools have enough money to buy new equipment, and have enough doctors and teachers. I also hope that the countryside stays nice and that people recycle more of their waste.

My fears for Scotland are that more and more young people will take drugs and not be healthy.

Scotland is a great country and I love living here.

by Alan Graham
P.6. Grandtully Primary School.

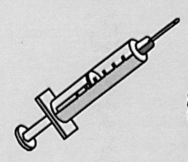

BONNI

BONN

Jody Kay Bramall and Kay Michelle McNab
Thornton Primary, Kirkcaldy

SCOTLAND

ESCOTLAND

35

Matthew Nicolson Aith Junior High School, Lerwick

Values

Values

The Elements

AIR
The cool, calm, gentle breeze,
Ripping apart, the autumn leaves,
Randomly groping, slashing, tearing,
Delicately soothing, clearly caring;

WATER
The shattering, smashing, seething waving,
Caresses the beach, tenderly engraving,
Uniting once more, with the silvery shore,
The sea revels, in splintering shells;

FIRE
The sun's warm enticing glow,
Absorbs the cold, with a licking swallow,
Intensely penetrating, engulfing, suffocating,
Hypnotically easing, relaxing enlightening;

EARTH
The earths green luscious pastures,
Human's interference, is unable to capture,
People revealed, but scenery concealed,
Witnessed by eyes, this devistation thrieves.

There will be peace on earth.
happiness for everyone.
endangered animals will be saved.
Millions of people will celebrate.
industry shall prosper.
Lonely people will have someone.
Lots of christmas carols.
everybody shall have good health.
new technology will be made.
new beginings for all.
i hope for friendships.
Underprivalaged children will have a chance
m.e will have a cure. By Megan Robertson.

Megan Robertson Muiredge Primary School, Uddingston

Family

I value my family because
family is really important to everyone

if you don't have your family
you will be lonely.

Martin Trainer Greenwood Academy, Irvine

THE LAST OF HIS KIND   BY MARA DOUGALL

When old Jo died the colony was shocked. I guess
we'd all forgotten he wasn't like us. You could tell he
was different from his appearance. He was frail and grey
in his old age. No one else on our planet or any
other planet was frail or grey or even old. Our hair was
built like synthetic fibres, its colour never fading, our
bones never broke for the scientists built us strong.
Old Jo had refused the artificial organs, probably
why he died. He said he didn't want to become
a robot and thats all we were.
They said he came about the old way. Born from a
woman, the last of his kind. Everyone said he
was mad but I liked old Jo and his old ways.

Mara Dougall, Oban High School

39

I hope i have no fear
of things i cannot hear
I fear i have no hope
And now i cannot cope

Names: Nicky callaghan
and Iain weir.
Ages: 11 and 11.
School: Grandtully primary school

Nicky Callaghan and Iain Weir
Grandtully Primary School, Pitlochry

Inner Voice

The saying "Children should be seen and not heard" gives adults more time to talk when they really have nothing important to say and children have a lot of important things to say but nobody will listen. A child can be screaming out for help but nobody can hear their inner cries.

I think children should rightfully be allowed to voice their opinions because there have been occasions when adults have had to rely solely on a child's information being truthful and accurate like in cases of domestic violence and murder charges when the only witnesses were the child and perpetrator.

Anne Franks diary was one of the first time adults had to admit defeat and allow a major event in history to be pictured through the eyes of a child who was in the middle of all of it. But still children are being ignored and treated unfairly. Now entering a new millennium will hopefully be protected and listened to more and forever more.

Jennifer Hardie Broughton High School, Edinburgh

My blood disorder

I have a blood disorder called hypofibrinogenaemia and there are only three people in Europe that has it. Well that is what my doctor said about two years ago so I don't know if there are any more people since then.

The disorder is a case of haemophilia, but it is worse in some ways. My blood does not clot right and I have to go to hospital if I am still bleeding for half an hour. I can't go straight to any hospital; I have to go to the hospital that I go to get my check ups and for my teeth. The hospital is YorkHill hospital for sick children. In Glasgow. If I cut myself and I have to go to hospital , on the way I will get a tablet to take and it will stop my blood going to the cut. If I take a heavy bang or a hit and I bruise straight away I will also have to go to hospital.

One time I broke my arm and I went the royal Alexander hospital in paisley and my mum got into trouble for not taking me to the right hospital. When I broke my arm it was weird because when I was running home someone asked me what was the matter. I took my hand off my arm and blood sprayed out of a very small hole in my skin. I broke a bone in three places.

I wish there was a hospital in Barrhead and a doctor that was trained to deal with my blood disorder so that I do not have to go away into Glasgow and take all that time when I could just take a few minutes if we had a hospital here.

I can't do a lot of sports with this disorder, I have tried to join a lot of things like trampolineing , football and rugby and things like that that. But no one will take me in because they are not qualified to do any thing if I fall and hurt myself. So please try to get a hospital and a nurse or doctor that can deal with my blood disorder quickly.

Andrew Murphy

Andrew, Barrhead

Making the Right Choice

This was a situation when I had to make the right choice between helping the old man or leaving him. In the end I think I made the right choice.

It was Halloween and I was going to meet my friend David. Then I saw an old man . First I thought he was drunk so I avoided him but he was coming towards me and said, " Help me I've been mugged!" Then he fell on me, got up, fell down again and hit his head off the wall. I asked what was wrong with him and he said that he had been mugged. So I ran to the nearest person and asked for help. He came over and looked at him. He said he needed stitches badly. So I ran to the nearest pay phone and called an ambulance. The ambulance came and took him away. When I was leaving the man that helped me said well done to me for my quick reactions.

Jamie Hooper

My Poem called (My Sisters problem)

I feel like I'm trapped Inside,
and all my childhood I have to hide,
If I stay here any longer,
My hate for them will grow stronger and stronger,
At seventeen and a child of three,
I cannot think of only me,
nowhere to run, nowhere to hide,
Only the streets and places outside,
I don't take drugs or even drink,
I can't do nothing not even think,
My life is taken over and so bad,
My child of three must feel so..so...sad,
I can't write or read,
and haven't even got what I need,
A place to sleep a child to love,
but the problem is my parents are so Rough,
I do have a job it's in a shop,
My child if she's Lucky she'll get a lollipop,
They give me a time for to be in,
If I'm not they put my dinner in the bin,
I really need help so open me in,
Don't Let me and my child live next to a bin,
I don't know what to do,
So please help me cos I havenae a clue,
        made up by
                Kirsty Hamilton   age 13
        Graeme High School . 2B1,

Kirsty, Falkirk

Important Qualities

Kindness
Kindness is like a flower that opens out fully to the sun.
Kindness is opening your hand and sharing with others.
Kindness is not holding back but giving.
Kindness knows no bounds.

Fairness
Fairness is like a perfectly accurate set of scale.
Fairness looks at both sides of an argument.
Fairness does not jump to conclusions.
Fairness avoids mistakes.

Honesty
Honesty is like an artist giving you all the details of his painting.
Honesty is telling all.
Honesty is not being unjust.
Honesty knows no lies.

Tolerance
Tolerance is like flowers growing together in one flower bed.
Tolerance is putting up with people who don't share your opinions.
Tolerance does not slam the door.
Tolerance endures everything.

Love
Love is like two flowers growing side by side.
Love cares and shares.
Love will not stop caring.
Love never quarrels.

Caring
Caring is like helping a lame beggar walk.
Caring is giving what you can.
Caring is not shrugging your shoulders.
Caring is helping a tree to grow.

Sharing
Sharing is like opening your hands to the world.
Sharing is dividing between lots of the poor.
Sharing is not ignoring the needs of others.
Sharing gives everyone joy.

ISLA MACLEOD-   PRIMARY 7

ME AND WHERE I LIVE

Hi, my name is Samantha Jay Rendall.
I'm eleven years old.I have four cats, two dogs and a
hamster.I live on a farm on which my family live ,we
look after sheep and cows.I always help in the
byre and slats.A byre is a big shed where
cows are chained up.The slats are pens
which fit 6-8 cows in each.I feed cows
hay,straw or silage.Orkney has a lot of
farms on the island.

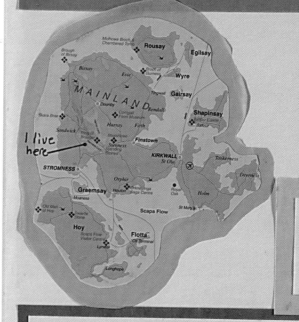

I live
here

My dre
grow u
My dre
money
with an

WISHES

I wish to carry on pl
my keyboard and vi
I wish I could have
animals to look afte
because I love all an

FUTURE SCHOOLS

In the future there will propably be more computers and that will
mean less paper.Everyone will be on the Internet and the schools
will probably use the internet instead of looking in books for
infomation.

HOPES

I hope Orkney
stays the same
and that the tourist
attractions will
stay the same.
I hope that we
can have a
shopping centre
in Kirkwall.
I hope that the winding
streets of Stromness
will stay the same.

Food in Orkn
Orkney
IceCrea

Lamb

Beey

Fish

Lobst

Samantha Jay Rendall Stromness Primary School, Orkney

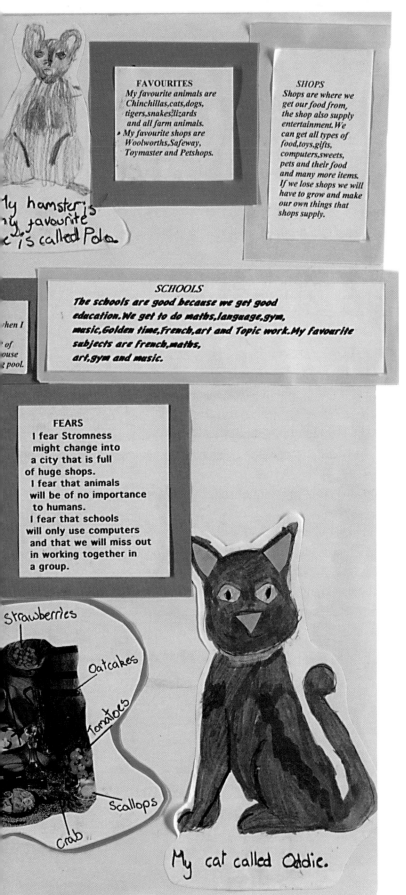

FAVOURITES
My favourite animals are
Chinchillas,cats,dogs,
tigers,snakes,lizards
and all farm animals.
• My favourite shops are
Woolworths,Safeway,
Toymaster and Petshops.

SHOPS
Shops are where we
get our food from,
the shop also supply
entertainment. We
can get all types of
food,toys,gifts,
computers,sweets,
pets and their food
and many more items.
If we lose shops we will
have to grow and make
our own things that
shops supply.

My hamster is
my favourite
... is called Pola

...hen I
... of
...ouse
... pool.

SCHOOLS
The schools are good because we get good
education. We get to do maths,language,gym,
music,Golden time,French,art and Topic work.My favourite
subjects are french,maths,
art,gym and music.

FEARS
I fear Stromness
might change into
a city that is full
of huge shops.
I fear that animals
will be of no importance
to humans.
I fear that schools
will only use computers
and that we will miss out
in working together in
a group.

Strawberries
Oatcakes
Tomatoes
Scallops
Crab

My cat called Oddie.

Listen!
Save The Children

My name is Laura-Jane Cameron. I go to Macmerry Primary School. My teacher is called Mrs. White.

My most valued thing to me is my Papa's teapot; he won it at his day care centre in the town nearest to Macmerry. Which is called Tranent.
He also gave me money to buy my locket bracelet, which is even more precious to me.

I really like my family because they give lots of things and comfort me. I live really close to my Granny and Granddad because they only live down the road from me. I don't get any pocket money because I usually get a magazine and some clothes every Saturday when my Mum gets the shopping. I don't have any brothers and sisters, so it's just Mum, Dad and me. My Mum is called Vera; she works for the East Lothian Council. My Dad is called Douglas, but he likes to be called Dougie instead. He works at Baush and Lomb, Livingston.

I don't think I argue with my Mum or Dad, but if I do they probably have a lot of tolerance.

My Mum and Dad have a lot of TLC. (Tender, Loving, Care) they give me big hugs when I am upset. Sometimes my Mum can get upset because of sad films, so I just give her the box of tissues.

My family is fair, but sometimes they are angry with me when I am late from coming in from the park when it was dark!

I really hope you enjoy my article on my family and me.
Good luck on your new project!

Laura-Jane Cameron

Problems

5

Louise Rankin Dalziel High School, Motherwell

Stuart Barnes Mauchline Primary School, Ayrshire

POVERTY UP BY 50% SINCE 1960!

DONALD DEWAR TAKES ACTION

The amazing rise in the number of poor and homeless people in Scotland has caused several problems, but has caused a record figure in the whole of Scotland, KLM Research stated last November.

If you go down Edinburgh's Princes Street any day of the week, you will see at least one person in a cardboard box, while if you go into Glasgow's poor area Possilpark, you will notice that there is at least one burning car on the street. Windows are boarded up and only a few very poor

A beggar on Edinburgh's streets Photo: Victor Gollancz.

people live in the messy flats that stand there.

There are by now so many people homeless in the whole of Scotland that it is impossible to totally wipe it out without spending billions upon billions of pounds on new housing for people with very bad or no housing.

Donald Dewar states in his recent speech, "With research carried out yesterday, we must take instant action on poverty and definitely homelessness."

"There are many people sitting out there in city centres in cardboard boxes, hoping to get money. We shall now help them!"

Citizens of cities have called in because they have seen 10 or 12 homeless people when they were out for their Saturday shopping.

A beggar who stays on a street in central Glasgow said to one of our reporters: "I am having to survive on one apple a day with the change of 2 pence pieces I receive from the people that go here every day."

Donald Dewar and Scottish Labour/Liberal Democrats are working to prevent any further poverty, but the poverty that exists will still get help.

Reporter - Christopher Lunn
Tel. 0141 283 9268

Christopher Lunn Trinity Primary School, Hawick

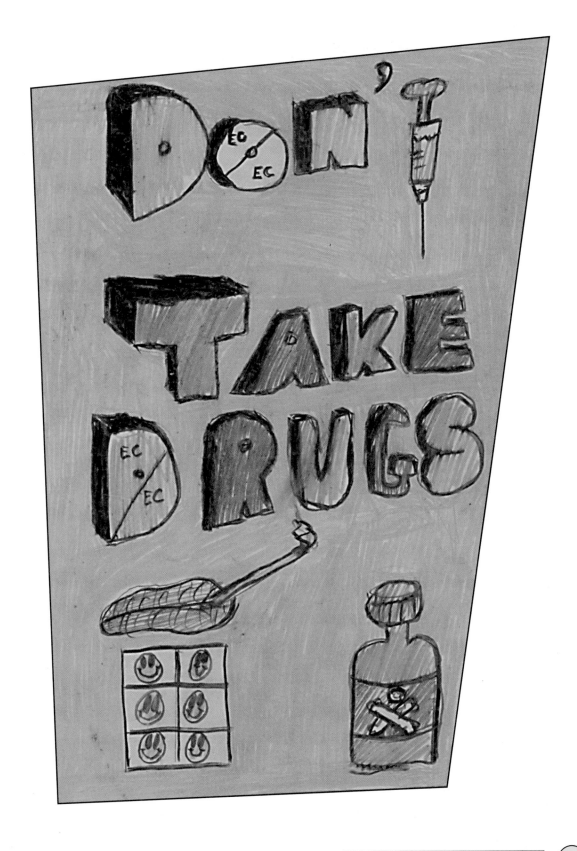

John Cumming Langbank Primary, Langbank

Drugs & thugs

Drugs and thugs are not good things,
They make your head go round in rings.

Tell a teacher or a friend they'll
help you out, in the end.

The police will catch them they'll
not fail and those drug dealers will
go straight to jail!

Johnnie Cunningham *Kirkcudbright Academy, Kirkcudbright*

Drugs

I think drugs are a serious problem.
Everybody knows this and they know it is harmful
but they are addictive and everybody knows that.
Some people will try hard to stop but others just don't care.

I think people take drugs because they are maybe stressed
or maybe they want to commit suicide.
Some people maybe take drugs because a friend has dared them.
If this did happen I don't think he/she was a real friend.

Most people think drugs and bullying and things like that
are down to boys, but it is not - girls do it as well.

I know someone who used to take drugs
and this has inspired me to write about this subject.
I prayed this person would stop. He was acting weird.

To anyone that does take drugs, please STOP!!

Smoking is bad for your lungs. It a

Cancer

William R Thomson *Thornton Primary School, Kirkcaldy*

ll you of give you lung cancer and throat

Drugs

Drugs are terrible things that kill millions of teenage people a year. Your first could be your last.

Pills, sniffers and needles are all very very dangerous and deadly things. These must all be banned to everyone not prescribed by the doctor.

Please help bann them!!!

Family

Familys are important and are always needed for support Yet not all families are together so thats what needs fixing.

by samantha Munro

Samantha Munro Fortrose Academy, Black Isle

A bottle of trouble

Chris: I think I'll go and see Jake.

(Ding-dong)

Jake: Hey Chris, What are you doing up?

Chris: Would you like to come up for tea.

Jake: I'll see if I'm allowed.

(Jake leaves)
(Jake comes back crying)

Jake: (sniff... sniff.) I'm not allowed (sniff...).

Chris: What happened?

Jake: (sniff... sniff.) Mam h-h-hit me-me (sniff...) She's (sniff...) drunk.

Chris: I'll go get dad!

(Chris gets Dad).

Dad: Where's your mother, Jake?

Jake: (sniff...) In the lounge.

(Dad goes into the lounge)

Dad: Calm down Julie. I'm taking this away.

(Dad took away vodka)

Julie: Ahh give arghh back...

(Julie collapses)

Dad: Dial 999 quick!

(The ambulance arrived)
(Julie came to)

Julie: What-t-t happened? I'm going to be sick.

Dad: Give up drinking. You're only hurting yourself and Jake!

Julie: Yes I will the hang-overs are not worth it.

(The End).

Jason Shand Aberlour Primary School, Moray

Picture It

Picture the Past
And the human race taking part in the breach of equality
Picture the Past
Where the whole world is in opposition to a different skin colour
Picture the Present
A revolution where a new generation finally protests
Picture the Present
The whole world's opinion changed so that no one is taken at face value
Picture the Future
A complete human race at harmony with each other

You never know, one day we might not have to picture it.

Philippa Hall

Philippa Hall **Oban High School**

Really hurtful remarks

A terrible description of coloured people

Criticising other people for their appearance

Ignorant remark towards coloured people

Stupid behaviour killing and death

Many people can't get a job because of this,
   this is called discrimination

David McCaig.

SPEAKING TO A RACIST!

Racism is not all about skin colour,
Its about belief,
Just because there skin colour is diffrent,
they're not underneath.

They grew up with a family,
Just like me and you
So in future,
think before you do.

You make them feel sad,
and very unwanted too,
all because you said,
I'm Better than You!

By
John Loughton.

John Loughton Broughton High School, Edinburgh

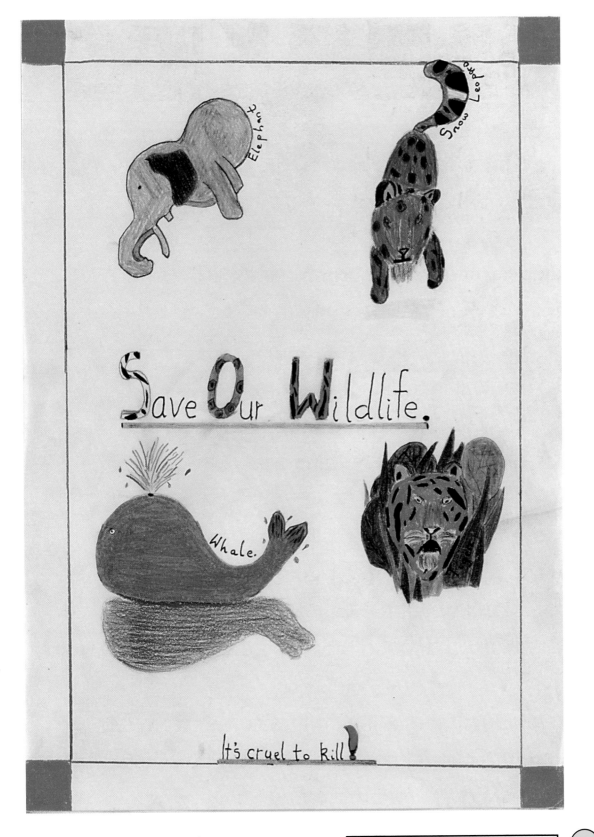

A NEW HOPE 2000

Stand up for the animals ,great or small,

Taking action, that is all,

Or showing that you care by stopping

Pollution that is killing

Animals, plants,and humans aswell,

Nearly all pandas are dead.

If we did not speak up for them,

Man would kill all living creatures,

Amazingly for their unique features.

Loving our world will help us all.

Children are the people of the future.

Raising your children to make them

Understand about the world.

Everyone could make the world a better place by doing

                                    things,

Like stopping the pollution that comes from us.

The future should be better ,for

You,me,and the nature around us.

Nicole Ross Trinity Primary School, Hawick

But what about tomorrow?

In the first decade of this century,
the world saw Mount Pelé erupt killing around thirty eight thousand people in St Pierre.

But what about tomorrow?

In the second decade of this century, the world saw two terrible world wars.

But what about tomorrow?

In the third decade of this century,
the world saw the rise of the Nazi Party and the start of the second world war.

But what about tomorrow?

In the fourth decade of this century, the world saw the horror of Hiroshima.

But what about tomorrow?

In the fifth decade of this century, the world saw the devastating effects
of the floods in China which left ten million people homeless.

But what about tomorrow?

In the sixth decade of this century,
the world saw one hundred and twenty thousand tons of oil into the sea, off Lands End.

But what about tomorrow?

In the seventh decade of this century,
the world saw the Tang Shan Earthquake kill seven hundred and fifty thousand people.

But what about tomorrow?

In the eighth decade of this century, the world saw the devastating effects of Piper Alpha.

But what about tomorrow?

In the ninth decade of this century, the world saw the tragedy of the Gulf War.

But what about tomorrow?

In the next century what will the world see?

What about tomorrow?

Imagine.

Ive been bullied three times but the most recent was the worst It was in Primary Seven. This one girl turned the whole class against me apart from one girl who she was bullying in the same way. Even my best friends didn't talk to me One girl had to mare school because of her

The school never did anything about it. They did speak to her but that didnt stop her - nothing did. It seemed as if it had happened overnight. One day I was friends with almost every one, the next I was alone with one person who spoke to me. The teacher knew it was going on but she did Nothing, Nothing at all.

I think in a way good has came from this I think I have more confidence and I have made lots of new, better friends that I hope will never do anything like that to me and I know I will never bully anyone and I hope teachers and parents do more to stop bullying in school.

Stacey, Barrhead

Bullying

TELL SOMEONE-BEFORE IT GETS TOO LATE

By Kimberly Ferguson P7

BY DIANE Campbell P7

Diane Campbell and Kimberley Ferguson
Laxdale Primary, Lewis

73

Donna Macmillan and Kerri Ann Mackenzie
Laxdale Primary School, Lewis

Y2k Rap

Don't be a dope and stay off the rope,
Because I know you won't cope.

If your being bullied, you know what to do,
Go tell your mum and dad, they'll sort it out with you.

When your mates are in a shop and they're getting ideas,
You do what is right and have no fear.

When your walking in the country drinking out the tin,
Keep in your hand then you chuck it in the bin.

Gary Dorans *Greenwood Academy, Irvine*

We could live better
life's without bullying

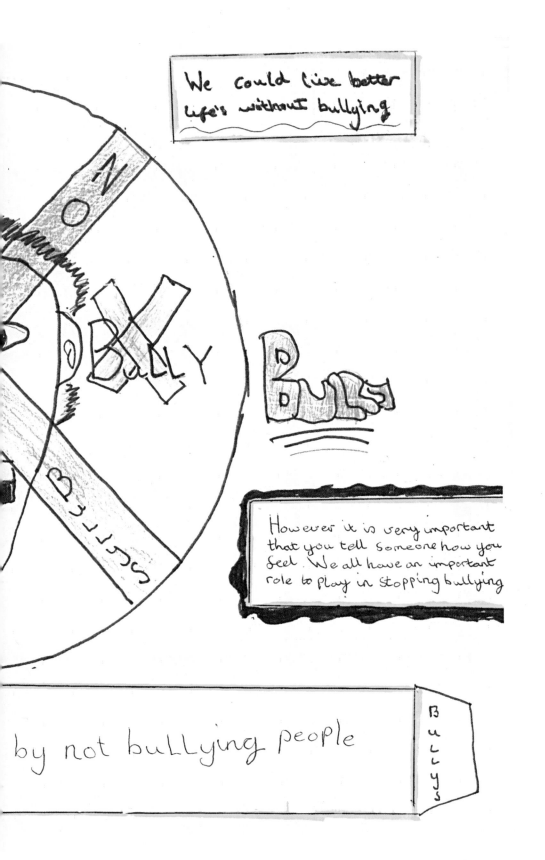

NO

BULLY

Bullys

Bullys

However it is very important
that you tell someone how you
feel. We all have an important
role to play in stopping bullying

by not bullying people

Bullys

Been tormented again today.

Until I almost cracked.

Lonely, and afraid no one would talk to me.

Like I am a leper or something.

You, stop this I told the bullies they just laughed,

cruel laughs.

Is there something wrong with me?

Nobody can help me.

Go away and leave me alone I scream inside my head.

They never will.

Anon, Edinburgh

Hopes and fears

My hopes for the future are that there are no people involved with drugs and drink because so many people are carrying a disease because they are adicted to drugs and drink.

My other hopes are for a cure for a different diseases like meningitis, Cancer, diabetine auds.

I also hope that I pass all my exams and get a good job I would like to be an artist or a machanic.

My last hope is for someday my mum will win the lottery because we could eat and drink as much as we like.

My fears are that the word is going t end on the millenium because I don't want to see it happen.

I also fear of being mugged at the age of 50 or 60 because it will be frightening and I wouldnotbe able to sleep.

My last fear is the global warming because it is melting the ice and could flood the world.

Kevin Muir

Relationships & your Community.
BULLYING.

There was once a girl called Kirstin. She was tall, blonde and English. The only problem was she had just moved to Scotland, since then she has had a totally different lifestyle because she gets bullyed. In Kirstins class there is another English girl called Leanne and she used to get bullyed about it all the time until she told someone. Leanne put up with the bullying for 5 months until the girls who were bullying got violent. In the end she had to tell someone, someone who she could talk to comfortably and someone she could trust. Leanne thought about who and finally decided to go to her guidance teacher. He asked quite alot of questions about what the girls were doing over the 5 months and who were bullying her. Leanne told him everything and the guidance spoke to them each individually and he told them that if it got any worse the police would be involved. The girls were scared and stopped bullying Leanne. Leanne can now get on with her life without being worried about getting hurt and bullied.
5 months Passed.
By this time Kirstin had settled in and was doing well at school until the girls who bullyed Leanne came after Kirstin because they were bored The girls first started with little messages But then the girls got so bad that they even

Holly Williams *Inverurie Academy, Inverurie*

put a cigarette out on her face. kirstin didn't know what to do so she went to Leanne and asked her what she did when they bullyed her. Leanne told her that she went to her guidance teacher. kirstin went away and thought about the message that she got which said if you tell anyone we'll kill you. kirstin was stuck in the middle.
She had 2 choices:

1. She could keep on getting bullied and it will ruin her life.
   or
2. She could tell her guidance teacher and the bullying would stop.

After alot of thought she finally made the right choice and went to her guidance teacher, she told him everything. Everything soon got sorted out and the bullying soon stopped. kirstin now can get back to her ordinary lifestyle like Leanne.
There is a message to this story:

IF YOU GET BULLIED TELL SOMEONE!

PROBLEMS AT HOME
by Joanne Leathern (2.b)

The door slammed. Lesley saw herself walking away from her problems once again. She knew that walking out wouldn't solve anything but this time it was the only thing she could do. Her dad had planned a family dinner for her younger brother Stephen, her father David and herself however, Caroline didn't need to come. What did she have to do with this family announcement?

Lesley patiently waited, trying to guess. Just after they had finished their meal, her dad said *"I have an announcement to make. Caroline and I, well, Caroline and I..."*

"Have decided to get married!" Caroline finished off. That's when she ran out of the house. She couldn't let them get married. Caroline couldn't take her mother's place.

"Where have you been young lady?" asked her father. *"I'm fourteen years old. I don't need to tell you where I'm going or where I've been"* Lesley shouted and then ran upstairs. *"Lesley, you come back here!"* she heard her father shout from downstairs. She ignored him and slammed her bedroom door only to discover Stephen in her room. *"What are you doing in my room? Get out now!"* she demanded.

"I'm sorry Les, I just wanted my C.D." he replied. "I didn't mean to shout. I'm just upset about dad marrying Caroline" Lesley said.

"It's going to be quite weird I suppose but we can't do anything about it" Stephen added.

"So where is she?"

"Who Caroline?"

"Yes"

"She went home about an hour ago"

"Do you think I hurt her feelings?" Lesley asked.

"I don't know but I need to go to bed" Stephen said "Goodnight Les".

"Goodnight" she replied. She lay awake for ages thinking about the wedding until she finally fell asleep.

Lesley came downstairs. Her father had cooked breakfast. She told him she wasn't hungry even although she was starving. She still wasn't happy but she was just going to have to accept it. "I'm going out" Lesley said.

"You can't go out without having breakfast" her dad said "Oh yes I can" she answered back.

"In fact you can't go out at all after the way you spoke to me last night. You're grounded!" her dad said. "Fine" Lesley shouted and once again stormed upstairs.

There was a knock on her bedroom door. It was Caroline. She wanted to speak to Lesley. Lesley let her in "Les, I know that me getting married to your father might have shocked you a little, and I know that you may not like me but we are still getting married and you will just need to get used to it" Caroline said.

Lesley knew that Caroline was right. After all Caroline wasn't that bad. "Caroline, I'm sorry for being so moody. It's not fair on you. I just need time to get used to this whole idea" Lesley said. A few tears slowly trickled down her face. "I keep thinking that you're trying to replace my mum" Lesley continued.

"I could never replace your mother but I would like you to respect me a little more". After Caroline said this her eyes filled up with tears. She was surprised when Lesley leaned over and gave her a hug. It was at that moment, when Lesley and Caroline settled their differences and began a new start.

Lesley, Stephen, David and Caroline got on as a real family and Lesley had a special place in her heart for her real mum Sandra.

Joanne Leathern Dalziel High School, Motherwell

One day I was playing with my friend Jaqueline
it was sunny and we were playing with the ball
and the ball landed on a used needle.

My friend didn't know the needle was under her ball
and she picked it up. We both went into the house and
washed our hands and all this happened in my back garden.

I don't play in my back garden anymore
my little brother Paul who is autistic could of gone out
and found the needle and injected himself.

If I was prime minister and I could pass one law
it would be no more needles in gardens.

There are two different forms of bullying. You can be bullied either physically or mentally, for example if you are bullied physically this usually means that the bullies push you around themselves, punch you, kick you, steal from you or call you names.

If you are bullied mentally this form of bullying usually includes the bullies talking about you behind your back, but maybe being nice to you when you are around.

Most people usually find out if they are being bullied in this form when other people who have overheard the bullies talking tell them.
I think this is the most hurtful form of bullying.

I'm sure that most people know at least one person who is being bullied, so the most important thing to do is to stay with them as much as you can. Try to get them to tell an adult about the bullying. Some people find it hard to tell their parents about their problems, so try and get them to tell a teacher, who can have a one-to-one talk with the bullies instead.

There are also a number of Childline Telephone numbers today and you can get these numbers from most magazines. The operator is not allowed to ask for any personal details such as your name and address or the names of the bullies, but will give you helpful tips on getting rid of the bullies.

Some bullies don't even realise how hurtful they are being towards other people. The bullies who do realise what they are doing are usually picking on people because they have no friends themselves and have nothing better to do. They are sometimes just coward's who want to act hard.

If you think you might be a bit of a bully, try thinking about the person or people you are bullying. How do they feel? What if they suddenly turn on you one day? It really isn't worth it.

Whether you or a friend are being bullied the best thing to do is tell an adult.

Donna MacMillan **Laxdale Primary School, Lewis**

Millennium/ Manifesto

6

Hopes for the future.

X-mas every Sunday?

for computers to do our school work.

Hello my name is Debra I am 10 years old and in primary 6. These are my hopes for the future. I hope it comes true. I come from Aberdeen and I speak Aberdonion. I am tall for my age and I have dark brown hair.

5x5 = 25 ✓
6x5 = 30 ✓
7x5 = 35 ✓
8x5 = 40 ✓

your pets can talk to you.

Hello   Hello

Wings so we could fly.

to travel around the world.

no more rain just sun.

for people to have food if they dont have.

for people to have clothes and trainer

Springhill

Debra 16/12/99

Debra Anderson *Springhill Primary School, Aberdeen*

Child of the Future?

A thousand years from now where you
live there may be:

A forest without trees, a concrete mass

heaving with dirt and pollution,
The Natural world Extinct, a huge black
hole lies where once a great city stood.
A dusty mist flies above this
tarmacked desert, no life, no feeling, except
for a small, pale, sickly child, the last
one of her kind left.
She sits at the top of a derelict
tower block, hiding in a corner, Dying of
Starvation, the melted remains of the shell
of a nuclear missile lies near a huge
crater,
The stupid creatures of this planet
destroyed themselves.
"And there's neooohh more war, cos there's
nooohh more world" the child hums
as shes tries to nurse the radiation
burns on her skinny limbs, she didn't
know what had happened when the
bomb hit the other side of the world.

Anon **Kirkcudbright Academy, Dumfries & Galloway**

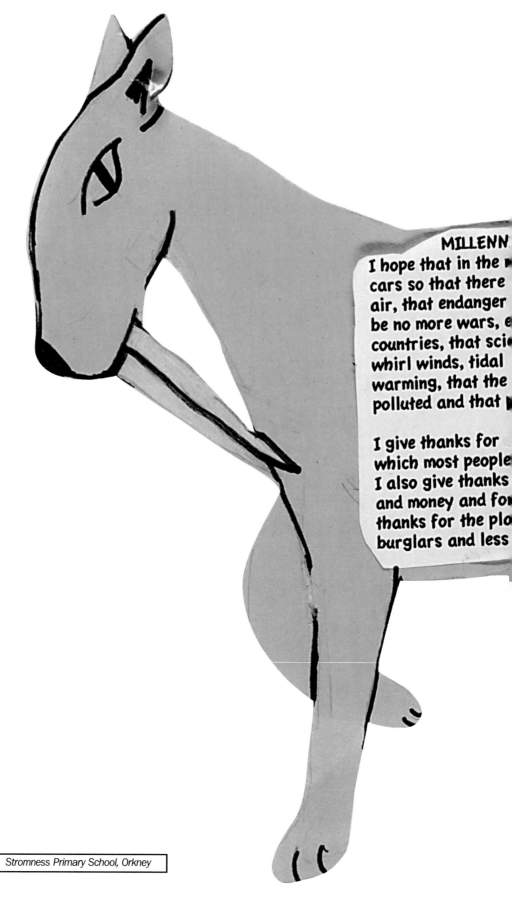

MILLENN

I hope that in the
cars so that there
air, that endanger
be no more wars, e
countries, that scie
whirl winds, tidal
warming, that the
polluted and that

I give thanks for
which most people
I also give thanks
and money and for
thanks for the pla
burglars and less

Ellen Walker Stromness Primary School, Orkney

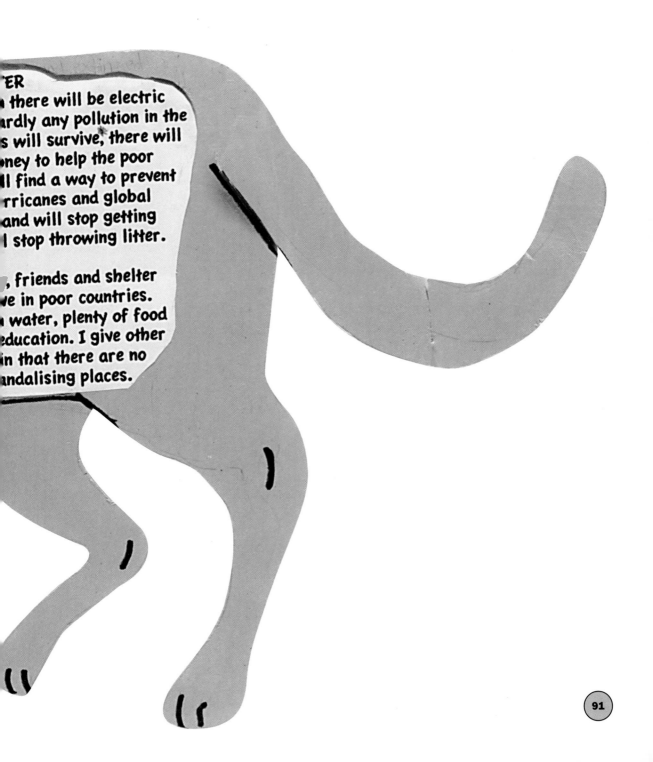

ER
there will be electric
ardly any pollution in the
s will survive, there will
oney to help the poor
ll find a way to prevent
rricanes and global
and will stop getting
l stop throwing litter.

, friends and shelter
ve in poor countries.
water, plenty of food
education. I give other
in that there are no
andalising places.

Colin Barrington Langbank Primary School, Langbank

I am Colin Barrington

I plan to be the next First Minister of Scotland and this how I am going to convince you that I am the one to vote for. Let me tell you the ideas I have if I am in charge and how I am going to make Scotland a better place for everyone.

You make think I am another man who says that he is the man to choose but I really am because I will take in everyones ideas and might even put them together to make a better idea so everyone has there own say on what they would like to see in the next couple of years.

In the next year or so, I would like to make your life a lot easier by cutting down on the tax that everyone has to pay because nearly everything you do there is tax on it, for example. There is tax for putting petrol in your car, electricity and heat to keep your house liveable, there is even tax just to put your car on the road. Sometimes I just want to hit that tax man with a hammer. So I would like to cut tax down by over 50%, but there is a bad side for smokers and drinkers because cigarettes and alcohol will go up by a minimum of 20%.

Colin Barrington *Langbank Primary School, Langbank*

My Manifesto for the Future
For The Isle of Lewis and The World

School

1) School will be a little bit shorter.
2) There will be really funky uniforms that everyone loves to wear.
3) Teachers don't keep you in if you haven't finished a part of your work.

Sport and Leisure

1) There will be a proper Lewis football league where big stars play and the managers pay millions for players to get transferred from another team.
2) There will be a huge adventure swimming pool, a bowling alley, an ice rink, a huge cinema and a roller coaster park with loads of fast rides.

Village and Community

1) There will be a train and tunnel under every road around the village.
2) The pavements will move up and down the road like a conveyor belt
3) The bus shelters will have comfy seats and will have doors and heating in them.

Space Aged Transport and Life

1) Cars can fly up into space, drive in water, hover, fly and drive on rough terrain.
2) Vehicles could get powered by normal tap water
3) We will be able to land and drive on the moon.
4) Everyone will have their own space shuttle, only a little one though.
5) We will be able to speak to aliens like a New World.

World

1) Everyone will have food and never be hungry again.
2) Drugs, cigarettes and guns will stop being made and sold.
3) War will end forever

By Angus Mitchell

Stacey Smith Greenwood Academy, Irvine

JENNIFER TARIQ PAMELA JONI CAMERON JA

JOSEPH GREGOR FIONA ASHLEY WESLEY LY

GARY DAVID ANGELA FREYA KENNY PHILIP

CARRIE ADAM GARY ANDREW STAN KEE

RHODA ROSS CALUM ERIM ANNA MARANIN

SARAH FIONA CATHERINE ISLAY LOUISE

CATRIONA JAQUELINE CLAIR FRASER M

KIERAN CATRIONA MELISSA COLIN NEIL

CALEIDH COLETTE JONATHAN CALUM ASHL

JAMIE JILLY STEWART INNES JAMIE AIDAN

BARBARA STEPHEN VICKY NICOLA ALLAN

ALLAN DONNA ALAN ALISON STEVEN DAV

EILIDH JAMES DAVID RHONA KAREN KI

GRAHAM DONALD MICHELLE KENNETH J

SEONAID DOUGLAS FINDLAY RENEE ARLENE

JONATHAN BEN STUART KELLY STEVEN GLO

PATRICIA STUART BERNEDETTE FIONA KAT

Stacey Felgate and Colette Lynagh
Oban High School

The millennium is in all of

LINE LISA DJ RICHARD SHELLY IAIN MARTIN
SAM DEBBIE STEPHEN CHERYL YVONNE IAN
LE KATY DONNA LYNN JENNA LIAM DAVID
NEILIDH JULIE BRIAN STUART VICTORIA
VIN CANDICE ANDREW STUART NAN DREW
PAUL LEANNA MARK MICHELLE ASHLEY
JOHN KAY LEIDH PHILIPPA JOHN IAN
DEBBIE CATHERINE JENNIFER SHARON SAM
OLIN ANDREW AILSA RYAN CLAIRE STACEY
STUART DUNCAN KATY EILIDH STEPHEN
E ANN-MARIE CRAIG CALLUM EILIDH ANN
AIRI EUAN PETER CRAIG STEWART GRAEME
TH CRAIG LAURA-ANNE DAVID DONALD
MARK STEVEN MICHELLE CHRISTOPHER
HEL ROBBIE SAMANTHA CAROL JAMES ALLAN
DUNCAN SARAH CAROLINE BARRY SHELLEY
ANOR FIONA SUSAN AMY FRASER MARTIN

in return we will all be in it!

Manifesto for the Millennium

- old people(60 and over) - should have stair lifts fitted. They need more help with heating bills. They should get free phone calls, TV licence and free prescriptions,bus and train passes.
- you should not have to pay for specialised wheelchairs (Like outdoor power chairs) - all wheelchairs should be free.
- equipment computers should be free to all pupils who need them to write with; also Talkers (communication aids) when they are needed . You should not have to try to raise the money
- access - we want to be able to go out when we want to. That means being able to get on any bus, train at any time. Now we have to make sure the bus has a tail lift and special tracks to clamp our chairs.
- there should be MUCH more room in ALL toilets, but especially disabled toilets
- all disabled toilets should have tracking hoists in the ceiling so we don't have to take our own hoists with us, just slings
- toilets in aeroplanes need to be bigger
- helpers should travel free and get free entry to activities when going with a disabled person
- more therapy in schools

What makes a good teacher ?

- good looking - a tidy appearance - hair not pink
- the opposite of proud - modest, interesting
- not a pain
- keeps a cool head, able to help, doesn't get angry, keeps their temper, does not swear
- lets you use the computer, play games, listen to music
- helps you when you ask for it
- a teacher with a bad attitude walks away - a good one lets you use your communication board, gives you time to communicate

Jenny Watt, Laura Smith, John Thompson,
Lynsey Rooney, Christopher di Paola **Corseford School, Glasgow**

Manifesto for the Millennium

☐ shops - make more room for wheelchairs

☐ access - to buses, trains, boats and planes - make them so we can get on without any bother

☐ stop the fighting in places like Kosovo - set up meetings, talks, Peace Talks, get food supplies

☐ homeless - give them money to get started, and find them somewhere to stay

☐ pay teachers, doctors and nurses more

The Competition

The dull melodious wail of the great pipe echoed over the seemingly
lifeless hills. A piper in full highland regalia stood dramatically on
the edge of a crag, a light breeze made his kilt flutter. The only other
form of movement was his fingers rythmically playing the tune and a
slight tap of his left foot keeping time. The music from the pipe did not
disturb the peace of the hills but somehow enhanced its richness and the
drama of the Scottish Highlands.
With small deliberate steps, the piper started towards the village
directly below the crag where he had been standing. Even in his regalia
he almost seemed part of the vast barren landscape.
Once in the village the piper broke into his favourite march from his
favourite place 'The Pap of Glencoe'. At a steady pace, the piper proudly
marched past the few shops and houses, the type which a tourist would
think of as a typical Highland village.
The piper stopped outside a cottage on the outskirts of the village,
carefully deflated his bag, opened the door and stepped inside.
Once inside the cottage, the piper found himself in a maze of colour and
warmth. There was the unique smell only associated with a peat fire and
the aroma of a pot of fresh broth bubbling away on top of the range
filled the room.
"Martin, is that you?" came a voice from another room.
"Yes mum," replied the piper in a voice that was much more quiet and
gentle than you would expect from a boy of his size.
"How was it?" came the voice, although a lot nearer this time.
"Cold and fantastic," replied Martin, as he put his pipes down on the
kitchen table.
"That's good then," murmured the voice, as the boy's mum came into the
room wearing an apron and dusting down the shelves with an emerald green
feather duster.
"Are you ready for tomorrow?" she asked smiling up at him because
although he was still young he was a head and shoulder taller than her.
"You can really show those amatuers how the great pipe should be played."
"Mum, don't boast," said the boy, picking up his pipe box as he left the
kitchen.
"I'm off to practice in my room," came the boy's voice from the top of
the stairs.
"Okay," replied Martin's mum as she carried on dusting.
Martin opened his bedroom door with his free hand. His room had an all
round mural of his favourite place, the Pap of Glencoe. On the floor was
a carpet patterned with the ancient MacDonald tartan and on the ceiling
were posters of solo pipers playing their pipes in Glencoe.
Flomping on his tartan clad bed and lovingly picking up his blackwood
practice chanter, like a mother picks up her newborn baby, he played his
entries for tomorrows local piping competition, 'The Pap of Glencoe',
'Maggie Cameron' and finally 'John Morrison of Assynthouse.' At last
satisfied with his performance he stopped playing. With big, but delicate
hands, he placed his chanter in its box and carefully put it next to his
bed.
He lovingly picked up his pipes, took them to pieces, rehemped the
drones, mouthpiece and chanter, put them together again and made sure
that they still sounded perfectly tuned. Putting his pipes back in their
box, he went down stairs and helped himself to a delicious bowl of fresh
homemade broth. Once he had eaten he returned upstairs.
Now safely back in the haven of his room, Martin put his kilt, jacket,
shirt, MacDonald tartan tie, socks and cleanly polished black shoes on
the back of a chair that was standing in the corner. Picking up his
chanter as before, he played all his favourite tunes. Time flew and

before long it was time for Martin to go to sleep. Setting his alarm clock and switching off his bedside lamp he fell into a dreamful sleep.

His radio blurted out Scottish accordian played reels on radio nan Gaidheal. Wearily, Martin dragged himself out of bed and into the bathroom to wash. Having woken up slightly, Martin returned to his room, donned his regalia and took himself and his pipes down the stairs and into the kitchen.

Munching over a bowl of cereal, he thought about what lay ahead of him that day. Putting his bowl in the sink, he checked in the kitchen mirror that he looked repectable, kissed his mum good-bye and started to walk the mile to the playing arena.

Once there, he got out his pipes, seasoned his bag and started 'tuning up'. Other competitors came in and looked inquisitively at the people who they were to compete against.

Before long, the loudspeaker called the competitors one by one 'to their doom'.

"Competitor number nine, Martin Beard," bellowed the megaphone.

Proudly picking up his pipes, Martin strutted up to the playing platform. He looked at the audience for anyone that he knew. Martin saw that his mum was sitting in the centre of the front row. He put the bass drone on his left shoulder, held the chanter top in his right hand, inflated the bag placed it under his oxter and struck up.

He started playing the march 'Pap of Glencoe' then strathspey 'Maggie Cameron' and finally his reel 'John Morrison of Assynthouse'. Martin repeated his three tunes, carefully deflated his bag and walked back to the tuning room. His mum was there to greet him.

"That was really great," enthused his mum.

"It's not a winner though," replied Martin "I played pretty well, but I made a few mistakes in 'John Morrison', I should hopefully come second or third. Angus should win it, as he was the best, even though he chose really simple tunes, but we will have to wait and see."

The last competitor walked off the platform, now it was in the lap of the gods, or judges as the case may be, to see who won.

"Due to the comparative difficulty of the tunes he chose to play, and the one or two minor errors made, we the judges have decided to award first place to Martin Beard of Barguillean," came the announcement over the loudspeaker.

In shock Martin collected his prize and waited for the other results. Angus came second and John MacIntyre third.

Martin gave his empty pipe case, trophy and prize money to his mum to take home for him.

One lone dark silhouette dressed in full highland regalia walked down to the sandy shore. In his hands he carried a stand of pipes. Playing his favourite tunes, Martin piped down the red gold sun on the deserted beach, utterly contented.

by
Martin Beard

Oban High School

Neil Braid and Jon Hutchison
Thornton Primary School, Kirkcaldy

DANNY

Mum! What's for breakfast? called Danny in the morning. Danny was always hungry in the morning but this day he had to do his history assignment on life in the past. Danny had arranged to go to the head museum to talk to some people from the year 2000. The head museum was a special gallery where old people's heads were preserved in a special liquid, in glass jars. The heads could talk, and could have perfect conversations with the person speaking to them.

They had been invented in the year 2080, 6 years before Danny was born. Danny was 14, and was quite fat. He had dark brown hair and bright orange eyes, which wasn't uncommon since that drug for pregnant woman had been invented. Danny's dad had died in a mining accident when he was five, so Danny had to do a lot of the housework while his mum was at work. His mum worked as a mechanic for teleporters, which transported people from one place to another.

Danny hated school, especially on Wednesdays. He had double history and triple maths. The half man - half machine teacher that he had was really grumpy, and always gave him more than a fair share of homework. He had got the history assignment that day, which wasn't as bad as the day before.

Danny's school wasn't really a school, because the teacher could be easily stored in the cupboard, so lived in his house. Most children had their own teacher, except for the people who lived in the slums or the outskirts of the city.

Danny's house had two bedrooms and was one of the more sophisticated homes in Rayton. Rayton was underground, the same as every city on Earth. The people had to move underground when a huge meteor was heading for Earth.

There was an international effort to stop it, but it didn't work, so the people made homes in the ground. Soon afterwards the meteor struck Earth with a frightening blow, and the population could not go back to the surface. They brought as many other living species as they could, but many had to be left, with a frightening blow, and the population could not go back to the surface. They brought as many other living species as they could, but many had to be left, and so became extinct. The people had got used to it, and now were perfectly adapted to living in the soil.

Once Danny had finished his breakfast of crunchy tasty Alieno's cereal and earth cakes, he said goodbye to his mum and stepped into the teleporter in the transport room. Danny typed in **HEAD MUSEUM** on the control panel and then pressed **GO**.

The experience of being teleported was very strange. You were warped into a tunnel with lots of bright, swirling colours and plenty of thick mist so that you couldn't see more than a few metres ahead of yourself. Danny loved the feeling of it all, but the journey only lasted around ten seconds, and your body could only be teleported once every two hours, because of the time you needed to get back to yourself.

Danny stepped out of the teleporter in the head museum and set out to do his work. While walking down the corridor in the museum, Danny bumped into his best friend, Craig Fenson. Craig was just there for a look around, since Craig's great grandad was 112, and had an almost immaculate memory for his age. He told him all about the world when he was a boy, and Craig had gathered all the information that he needed.

Danny told Craig what he was about to do, and he thought it was great idea. They said goodbye to each other and Danny carried on to the main room towards the heads. When he reached the room Danny looked around. There were hundreds of heads, but he decided to go to someone relatively young because they would have a better memory. People only got their head put in a jar if they wanted to and it only happened if you were dead, like if you had been killed by unnatural death. Danny spotted what he thought was the right one. Her name was Lucy, and looked like she was in her late teens. Danny went up to her and asked if he could talk to her. She said yes.

So Danny said *"What was life like living above the ground?"*

Lucy knew he would ask that question. *"Completely different. There were no teleporters in those days, so people mainly got around on foot and in cars."*

"Cars?", Danny had never seen cars, they were unusable underground.

"Yes." said Lucy. *"They had four wheels and an engine, and you controlled them with a steering wheel. Only 5 people could go in them at a time. There were lots of other ways of transport too, but I cannot possibly say them all."*

"Okay, so what did people do for fun?"

"Well most people played sports or had a computer with games, there were no V.R. games or grav-ball to play, as they weren't invented."

"Interesting, but it sounds a bit boring. Anyway, what was it like living with animals?"

"Well a lot of people had pets, like a dog, cat or hamster, and there were a lot of birds flying in the sky."

Danny and Lucy talked about lots of things and once he had got all the information that he needed he said thank you and waved goodbye to Lucy. Of course Lucy did not wave back as she only had a head and it is quite hard to wave without arms.

The next day Danny's history teacher, Mr Past, was very glad to see Danny's report. He even stored it on his long term memory. Danny was very glad he had picked Lucy as she had been very helpful and he hoped to see her again.

JUSTICE AND FAIRNESS

There are many different points to consider when speaking or writing about justice and fairness. Legal rights, police and equality are only a few of many.

In courts, many people receive a suitable punishment for the various crimes they commit. There are also many who do not get a punishment severe enough.

Rich people could afford a great lawyer who would make the judges believe that an easy punishment would be suitable when it is not.

Convincing liars could also be given a punishment many people would consider unsuitable. I do not think that doing a terrible crime should be rewarded in this way. Judges should be trained more efficiently so that they know who is lying. Celebrities also are given punishments which are easy simply because they are famous.

The Law should apply to everyone, famous or not.

I think that policemen and policewomen should be trained more efficiently. Many police officers do not investigate even the smallest house calls. Some of these calls are serious, like disruptive people fighting, but police reach the area late, giving the people time to hide the weapons (evidence). This would be okay if the police investigated the scene, but they do not. If they did, these people would be put away, allowing people to actually enjoy living where they do rather than hating their neighbourhoods.

I think that there should be equality for everyone. Many terrible people are racist, which is even worse if they are employers, leaving people unemployed. This is disgraceful as people who have talent are left with nowhere to use it. The same goes for male and female equality. We are all human, after all.

I hate the way that young people are treated, particularly by shopkeepers. A thirty year old man could walk into a shop and around the aisles very easily.

If a thirteen year old boy walked in and around the same store, the owner would watch him every step, or even follow him. This can feel very uncomfortable I would have thought that an adult can cause more trouble, but shopkeepers seem to think otherwise.

I believe that there are many things which need to be changed in order to make our society a more just and fair one.

**Pauline Heffron
2 DHI.**

Pauline Heffron Barrhead High School, Barrhead

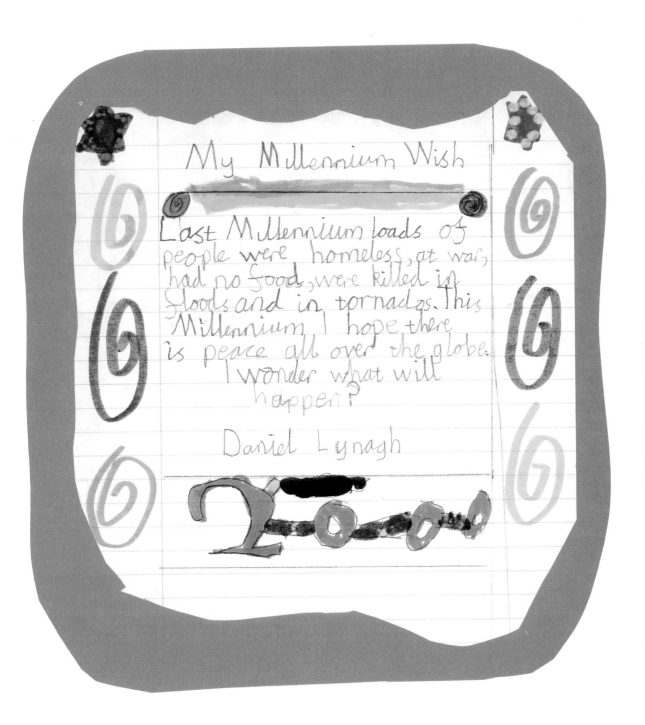

My Millennium Wish

Last Millennium loads of people were homeless, at war, had no food, were killed in floods and in tornados. This Millennium I hope there is peace all over the globe. I wonder what will happen?

Daniel Lynagh

2000

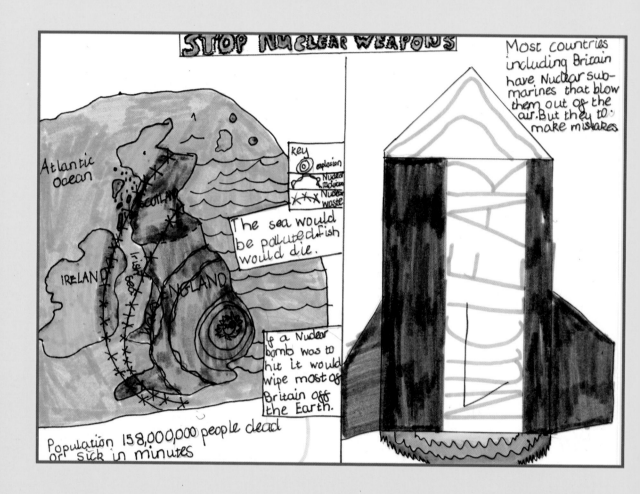

Ian Black **Mauchline Primary School, Ayrshire**

If for one day

If for one day,
I was ruler of the world,
I'd think of all the problems,
and how they could be solved.

If for one day,
The homeless could have homes,
The poor could have money
and no more debts and loans.

If for one day,
Those in drought could have rain,
Those in hunger could have food,
Those in hospital, no pain.

If for one day,
The world could have peace,
No weapons, no fighting,
and all was at ease.

I wish, I wish, I wish,
Everyday could be like this.

Martha Clark *Broughton High School, Edinburgh*

My Millennium Wish

I wish that the new Millennium made no more wars or fights. I also wish that everyone was kind in the world.

Amen.

Ainslie. P.4A

Ainslie Keenan St Matthews Primary School, Bishopbriggs

Visions of the future

January 5th 1999

Dear Diary,

I was woken this morning by the radio. Chechnya has been bombed again. I wish the world was at peace. Maybe it will be different in the future.

I spilt milk down my tie and nearly missed the bus in attempt to clean it up. The postman delivered the bills as I was leaving. I hope Dad gets a job soon so we can pay them all. Life's been hard since he was made redundant.

The bus nearly broke down on the way to school because it was so cold. But that just gave me more time to finish the Maths homework I had forgotten to do. These bloomin' equations!

Anyway, I saw Jack today. He is sooo cute. Maybe I'll see him at the Christmas dance.

Went out for lunch with Gemma today. They sell lovely hot fresh bread in Tesco. Mmmm!

Our History teacher was off today so we got some stupid supply teacher who didn't know anything. And talking of History, the Queen is coming to open a museum just up the road on Saturday so I might go with Alice to see that.

When I got home Dad told me he had been to the Job Centre and applied for a job so we got Chinese takeaway to celebrate.

Gemma is going to Australia in the Easter holidays. I don't think we'll be going anywhere for a few years but I would really like to go to America one day.

Well I've got to go but I'll write tomorrow

Luv
Susan.

Fiona Beaton and Sarah Thomson
Oban High School

January 5th 2100

Dear Diary,

I was woken this morning by Z2 our robot shaking me, apparently our new president has scrubbed 3rd world debt. The virtual phone was on the blink again so I had to e-mail my essay to school this morning, which is a pain because it's so slow.

Lorna and I were almost late for school this morning she spilt milk on her tie and she insisted on using the washing machine rather than the turbo stain presser . Then I got into a row with Mum over the virtu - phone bill , maybe I have been using it a bit much recently. It was sunny today which means we could get the solar bus , it's so much more comfy than the windpowered bus which is so old its falling apart. There was a new boy on the bus this morning he is sooo cute and he's in my class too!

At lunch time we fought the crowds and got a table on the canteen balcony. I don't know why the school insists on cooking the meals when so many places these days have those machines where you request anything and pop! Out it comes. In Modern studies our teacher was ill so his clone came instead , we learnt all about how England is debating getting a president like Scotland. I bet the King isn't happy about that! This afternoon I left my palm-top in psychology meaning I had to WRITE all my notes for Chinese, maths and finance I'll never catch up.

After school I discovered Dad has found a job, the employee machine finally matched his qualifications with something. When we got home he had the dinner ready he'd ordered straight from India by the virtu- phone I love when we do that . Unfortunately the war is still on in America I wish people wouldn't fight but it was supposedly worse in the 1990's . Lorna hogged the virtual reality machine all night. Just when I get a new disk for it it's called underground explorer. Maybe now Dad has a job we'll go to Mars or the Moon this summer my friends have been and they all loved them we usually just go to somewhere like Spain which is okay but I'd tan better on Mars.

I'll write tomorrow
luv
Mairi

3D TV over
channels at the
— click of
bu

who
knows what
the future
will hold,
we may even
have invented
virtual school,
or even virtual holidays.

We might be able to
buy anything on the computer and have it
driven to our door by computers.

Instead of a drive-in,
McDonalds could come
to you.

GOO
POIN
ABOU
THE FUTU

We may
have invented
cheaper way of runnin
our car instead of
petrol, who knows
someone may have even
invented a car that runs
on water.

The technology might be so advanced that there would be computers or robots to do the work, so it would be harder to get a job.

Everyone will be overweight because computers would have been invented to do everything for us.

They may have even shown every episode of Jerry Springer. Ha Ha!

BAD
POINTS
ABOUT THE
FUTURE!

Jet-powered
FOOTWEAR!!

THE

LATE FOR A
PARTY, DON'T
DESPAIR, TRY ON
OUR NEW ROCKET
POWERED FOOTWEAR!!!!

Nobody really knows what what
more advanced so who knows what kin
with. We might be flying our cars to
any sort of meal you want in a tablet
certain diseases. We might have prevente
the future might not be that different
Sometimes you have to stop and wonder wh
things and recycle things but what about th
build up to huge ammounts so then what
we could have invented some way of get

Flying car with solar
pannels on the wings
to power the engine.

Jet-powered shoes

A cheaper way of getting
anywhere and no petrol
expences.

Far
the ax
that it
layer o
we ma
own wa

This poster was created
Sylvie Foster and

Sylvie Foster and Jennifer Willing
Perth High School

...URE

...bring. Technology is becoming more and
...inventions people could have come up
...maring edible clothes or we could have
...ter in the future we could have cures for
...rom getting ill altogeather. Then again
...e there would be a few changes but not many.
...rubbish going to go. Of course you could burn
...couldn't burn or recycle it would gradually
...about it? Would we dump it in space? Or maybe
...? Who knows.

The Year

2222!!

...e future
...be so polluted
...e a permanent
...round it. And
...swimming in our

...ar 2000, by
...ling both aged 12.

Edible clothes
could be a major
fashion item and a
very tasty outfit!

Edible clothes could
be a lot cheaper because
you wouldn't be buying them
from a designer shop, you
would be buying them from
supermarkets.

my vision of the future

Hello my name is Dale Mackintosh. I am 10 years old. I come from aberdeen. If I was thinking of the vision of the future I think ther should be a special park there will be an a Electricl Sea-saw and a Jet swing and a Magic climbing frame and across from that there will be a carnival with a magic Roller coster and flying dodgems and an under ground ghost train and a Real plane trip and a magic boat that goes to sea this will all be in a special building. If your mum and Dad are arguing or if your mom and Dad are in hospital or if they are out for a meal or something there is something-else. A Magic museum there is old fashiond cars. and old boats and old police suits but now I will tell you what I think the magic will be there will be a special remote control that will make everything move on a track and I think it will be amazing Everybody will think it is exiting theyre will be everything in this building it is amazing the End by Dale Mackintosh

Dale Mackintosh Springhill Primary School, Aberdeen

Our Shrinking world   By Findlay Ross 3H Oban High School

FINDLAY	Nan, guess what?
NANA	What, son?
FINDLAY	The world is getting smaller.
NANA	No it's not, it's the same size it was last year.
FINDLAY	No really, the world is getting smaller.
NANA	Oh, is it? I hadn't noticed. I bet it's that millennium bug or global warming!
FINDLAY	No, but I'll give you a clue, the cause of it is in my house and just about everyone else's in Britain.
NANA	I haven't got a clue, what is it?
FINDLAY	It's the internet!
NANA	What net are you talking about? I don't have any net!
FINDLAY	No! The *INTER* net. It's a thing on the computer!
NANA	Oh, I see. Well how is this Internet making the world smaller?
FINDLAY	Well lets see........Instead of going down to visit your friends at their house, you could talk to them in an Internet chat room. Or instead of going into Glasgow to buy yourself a new T.V. you could order one from one of the shopping websites *and* have it delivered to your door!
NANA	Well, that sounds very nice, but how is it making the world smaller?
FINDLAY	You see, the thing with the internet is that the world is literally at your fingertips. For example, a couple of months ago I got in touch with people from France, Belgium, Poland, and Finland. You can do just about anything on the internet ;- You can find a job, Buy a new house or even just find out the latest football scores. It's amazing!
NANA	And all this is in your house Findlay?
FINDLAY	Yes, and it's great!

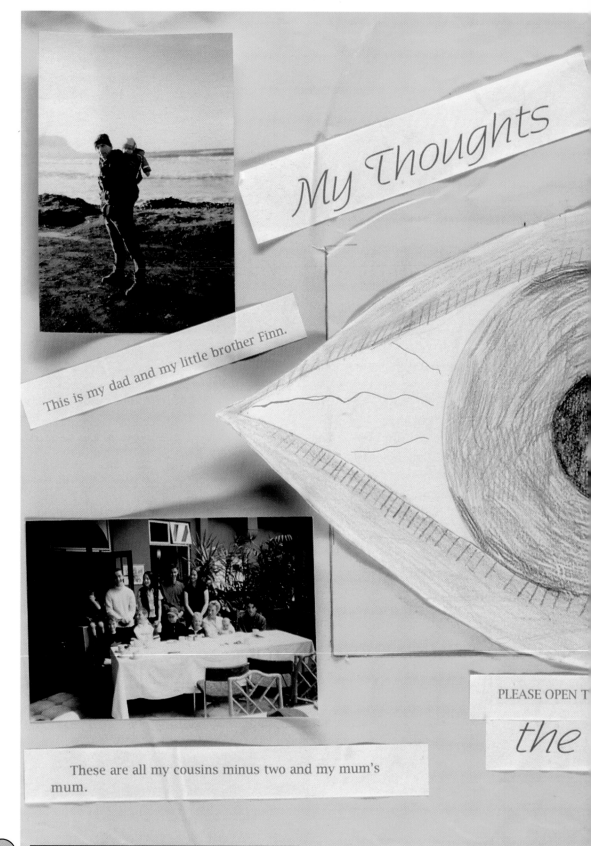

My Thoughts

This is my dad and my little brother Finn.

These are all my cousins minus two and my mum's mum.

PLEASE OPEN T

the

Niamh Anne Delaney Stromness Primary School, Orkney

d Visions for

This is my mum and my Gran.

ND MY WRITING

ure

This is a picture of the town where I live.

My view of the Future

I think that in the future there will be something strange happening. Whether it is a new world under the sea or a new world in Mars. It might in our world or any thing. But that's just my opinion!

Nicola McGill *Barrhead High School, Barrhead*

Aberlour Primary School, Moray

Airidhantuim Primary School, Isle of Lewis

Aith Junior High School, Shetland

Article 12, Dundee

Barrhead High School, East Renfrewshire

Bressay Primary School, Shetland

Broughton High School, Edinburgh

Corseford School, Renfrewshire

Craigie High School, Dundee

Dalziel High School, Motherwell, N. Lanarkshire

Drummond High School, Edinburgh

Dumbarton Academy, West Dunbartonshire

Ellon Primary School, Aberdeenshire

Fortrose Academy, Black Isle

George Watson's College, Edinburgh

Glasgow Braendam Link

Graeme High School, Falkirk

Grandtully Primary School, Pitlochry

Greenwood Academy, Irvine, North Ayrshire

Hermitage Primary School, Helensburgh, Argyll & Bute

Inverurie Academy, Aberdeenshire

James Gillespie High School, Edinburgh

Kirkcudbright Academy, Dumfries & Galloway

Lady Alice Primary School, Greenock, Inverclyde

Langbank Primary School, Renfrewshire

Laxdale Primary School, Isle of Lewis

Leith Primary School, Edinburgh

Lochmaben Primary School, Lockerbie, Dumfries & Galloway

Loirston Primary School, Aberdeen

Lornshill Academy, Alloa, Clackmananshire

MacMerry Primary School, Tranent, East Lothian

Mauchline Primary School, East Ayrshire

Moray Primary School, Grangemouth,

Muiredge Primary School, Uddingston, Glasgow

Oban High School, Argyll & Bute

Perth High School

PHAB/Royal Blind School, Edinburgh

Shakti Women's Aid, Edinburgh

Springhill Primary School, Aberdeen

St Matthews Primary School, Bishopbriggs

St Thomas of Aquins, Edinburgh

Stromness Primary School, Orkney

The Corner, Dundee

Thornton Primary School, Kirkcaldy,

Trinity Primary School, Hawick

Upper Annandale Youth Support Group, Moffat.

Viewforth High School, Kirkcaldy

West Calder High School, West Lothian

Acknowledgements

There were over 1400 creative contributions from children in 48 schools and groups across Scotland.

We also received over 2000 responses to the questionnaire *A Portrait of Your Life at 2000*, included with the Campaign.

Save the Children was delighted to have received such a high standard of material and our thanks to all the children and young people who took the time and trouble to create such a memorable Campaign.

We would also like to thank all the teachers in the participating schools who introduced the subject areas in class to get everyone started and were so positive in their support for the *Million Children* Campaign.

Save the Children gratefully acknowledges the support and assistance of the following companies and individuals in successfully completing the *Million Children* Campaign.

Rose Watban, and **Maureen Barry** at the Museum of Scotland in Edinburgh who have worked with us throughout the project

Dr Lynn Abrams, University of Glasgow and **Professor Chris Turner**, who advised us on the questionnaire, *A Portrait of Your Life at 2000*

Fraser Lumsden, Craig Lumsden. David Brunton, Gayle Smith and **John Anderson** at A.W. Lumsden, Craft Bookbinding who produced *The Declaration of the Million Children of Scotland 2000*

Allison Traynor, Iain Lauder, Jason Little, Kevin Greenan and **Nikki West** at Redpath for the design and production of the Campaign's launch materials

Anna Isola Crolla, Ryan Singh and **Elina Beswick** for the Campaign's launch image

Dr Murray Simpson at the National Library of Scotland in Edinburgh where all the original material from the Campaign will be archived

Alex McSherry, David & Mark Barnes, Ian Burden and **Jim Mason** who helped us on the Campaign's Launch Day

Antonia Reeve for the Campaign events photography

The Yellow Pencil Company who undertook the design and production of The Declaration, exhibition and paperback as well as the project's schoolpack and teaching guide

Eastern Display who produced the *Million Children* exhibition material

Elizabeth Henson and **Robin McTaggart** at The Multimedia Team who designed the *Million Children* Campaign web pages

Hannah Firth, David Kennedy, Fiona Henderson, Marc Lambert, Ewan MacVicar, Catherine Lockerbie, Emma McTaggart, Anne Campbell, Derek Cadogan and **Sylvia Dow** who were our judges for the various written and visual categories

Katrena Allen and **Margaret Sharp** at Glowworm Books.

Prizes and gifts in kind were donated by: